PIANO SOLO

SWEET SONGS OF
Christmas

SEASONAL ARRANGEMENTS

BY JOHN LEAVITT

ISBN 0-634-01821-3

BROOKFIELD PRESS

EXCLUSIVELY DISTRIBUTED BY

7777 W. BLUEMOUND RD. P.O. BOX 13819 MILWAUKEE, WI 53213

For all works contained herein:
Unauthorized copying, arranging, adapting, recording or public performance is an infringement of copyright.
Infringers are liable under the law.

Visit Hal Leonard Online at
www.halleonard.com

CONTENTS

A CD RECORDING OF THE ARRANGEMENTS IN THIS BOOK IS ALSO AVAILABLE (HL08742518).

SWEET SONGS OF Christmas

Dr. John Leavitt is one of the new, energetic young faces to emerge on the music scene. During the past fifteen years he has served as a clinician or conductor for hundreds of concerts, festivals and workshops throughout North America. Dr. Leavitt has been a regular guest on the MidAmerica Productions Carnegie Hall Series and will return to Carnegie Hall in June of 2000 to conduct the premier of his "Requiem." Dr. Leavitt is also a frequent guest recitalist on both piano and organ throughout the Midwest.

Dr. Leavitt has won a decade of consecutive ASCAP annual awards for his compositions and arrangements, which have been performed across the globe including North and South America, Europe, Australia and Japan; and his music has been featured on many North American broadcasts. Most recently, his "Scenes of Childhood" for organ has been featured on American Public Radio's "Pipedreams." His arrangement of "A Mighty Fortress" serves as the signature theme for the weekly national broadcast of "The Lutheran Hour."

Dr. Leavitt has also built an impressive discography. His recordings include "Simple Gifts," original piano works played by the composer, (1995); "River in Judea," original choral works conducted by the composer (1995); "Christmas Gift," piano (1996); "A Sonic Spectacular," organ (1997); "A Little Night Music," piano (1998); "Handel's Messiah," choral (1998) and "Sweet Songs of Christmas," piano (2000).

A native of Kansas, Dr. Leavitt was born and raised in Leavenworth. In 1990 he completed doctoral work in conducting at the University of Missouri-Kansas City Conservatory of Music. Dr. Leavitt also holds a Master of Music degree from Wichita State University (KS) in piano performance with additional emphasis in composition. His undergraduate work is in music education from Emporia State University (KS).

During and following the completion of his doctorate, Dr. Leavitt served as a faculty member in the music department at Friends University (KS), where he received the faculty award for teaching excellence. In the fall of 1992 he accepted a one-year teaching appointment with Concordia College in Edmonton, Alberta in Canada.

In 1993 Dr. Leavitt returned to Wichita where he continues to concentrate his efforts on composing, conducting and lecturing, as well as performing with his wife Connie, sons Matthew and Christopher, and daughter Katy.

Dr. Leavitt's other responsibilities in Wichita include serving as artistic director and conductor of the professionally trained vocal ensembles known as The Master Arts Chorale and Youth Chorale, which he founded in 1990. Under his direction, The Master Arts Youth Chorale was featured in performance at Carnegie Hall, St. Patrick's Cathedral and NBC's "Today Show" over Thanksgiving weekend of 1999. The Master Arts Adult Chorale will premier his "Requiem" at Carnegie Hall in June of 2000. He also serves as Cantor (director of the parish music program) at Reformation Lutheran Church in Wichita, Kansas.

For Matthew

Angels We Have Heard on High

Traditional French Carol
Translated by JAMES CHADWICK
Setting by JOHN LEAVITT

Copyright © 2000 by HAL LEONARD CORPORATION
International Copyright Secured   All Rights Reserved

no pedal

with pedal

dim. e rit.

(sost. pedal)

For Mom

Away in a Manger

Traditional
Words by JOHN T. McFARLAND (v.3)
Music by WILLIAM J. KIRKPATRICK
Arranged by JOHN LEAVITT

Copyright © 2000 by HAL LEONARD CORPORATION
International Copyright Secured   All Rights Reserved

To Coda

For Katy

Bring a Torch, Jeannette, Isabella

17th Century French Provençal Carol
Arranged by JOHN LEAVITT

Gracefully, with expression   (♩ = c. 42)

Copyright © 2000 by HAL LEONARD CORPORATION
International Copyright Secured   All Rights Reserved

14

For Kristin

A Christmas Garland

A Medley of "Ring, Merry Bell,"
"Still, Still, Still" and "O How Joyfully"

Traditional German Carols
Arranged by JOHN LEAVITT

Kling, Glockchen (Ring, Merry Bell)
German Folk Carol

Copyright © 2000 by HAL LEONARD CORPORATION
International Copyright Secured   All Rights Reserved

18

Still, Still, Still
Salzburg Melody, c.1819

Peacefully (♩ = c. 76)

With ebullience! (♩ = c. 94)

O How Joyfully
German Words by Johannes Falk
Traditional Latin Melody

For Dad

Ding Dong! Merrily on High!

French Carol
Arranged by JOHN LEAVITT

Copyright © 2000 by HAL LEONARD CORPORATION
International Copyright Secured   All Rights Reserved

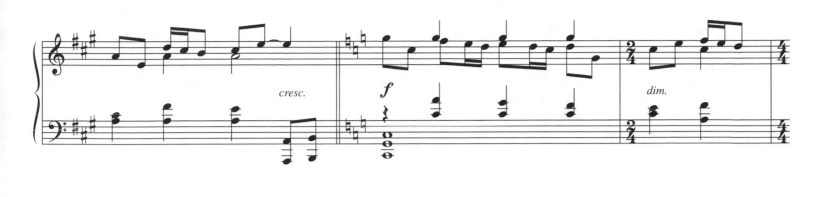

For Nina

In the Bleak Midwinter

Poem by CHRISTINA ROSSETTI
Music by GUSTAV HOLST
Setting by JOHN LEAVITT

Dolce e cantabile (♩ = c. 72)

Copyright © 2000 by HAL LEONARD CORPORATION
International Copyright Secured   All Rights Reserved

To Coda ⊕

D.S. al Coda

CODA

rit.

8va

Ped.

For Joe

Infant Holy, Infant Lowly

Traditional Polish Carol
Paraphrased by EDITH M.G. REED
Arranged by JOHN LEAVITT

Sweetly, with freedom (♩ = c. 72)

Copyright © 2000 by HAL LEONARD CORPORATION
International Copyright Secured   All Rights Reserved

For Connie

O Little Town of Bethlehem

Words by PHILLIPS BROOKS
Music by LEWIS H. REDNER
Arranged by JOHN LEAVITT

Tenderly, with freedom (♩ = c. 82)

Copyright © 2000 by HAL LEONARD CORPORATION
International Copyright Secured   All Rights Reserved

D.S. al Coda

CODA

dim. e rit.

p a tempo

rit.

For Lance

Resonet in laudibus

Let the Voice of Praise Resound

14th Century German Carol
Arranged by JOHN LEAVITT

Copyright © 2000 by HAL LEONARD CORPORATION
International Copyright Secured   All Rights Reserved

For Christopher

What Child Is This?

Words by WILLIAM C. DIX
16th Century English Melody
Arranged by JOHN LEAVITT

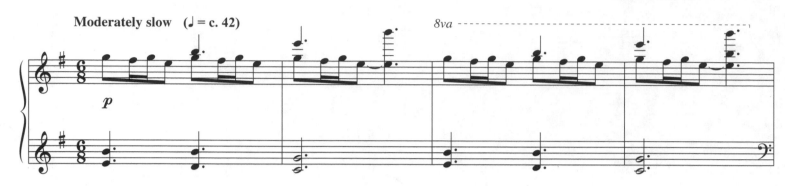

Copyright © 2000 by HAL LEONARD CORPORATION
International Copyright Secured   All Rights Reserved